KU-298-425

# Working with wood
# Background information

A Unit for teachers

PROFESSIONAL STUDIES CENTRE
EDUCATION FACULTY
BATH COLLEGE OF HIGHER EDUCATION
NEWTON PARK
BATH
BA2 9BN

Published for the Schools Council by
Macdonald Educational, London and Milwaukee

First published in Great Britain 1972 by
**Macdonald Educational Ltd**
Holywell House, Worship Street
London EC2A 2EN

Macdonald-Raintree Inc.
205 W. Highland Avenue
Milwaukee, Wisconsin 53203

Reprinted 1973, 1976 (with amendments), 1980, 1981

© Schools Council Publications 1972

All rights reserved. No part of this publication may be reproduced, stored in a retrieval system, or transmitted, in any form or by any means, electronic, mechanical, photocopying, recording or otherwise, without prior permission of the publishers.

ISBN 0 356 04010 0

Library of Congress Catalog Card Number
77-82995

The chief author of this book is:

Sheila Parker

The other members of the Science 5/13 team are:

| | |
|---|---|
| Len Ennever | Project Director |
| Albert James | Deputy Project Director |
| Wynne Harlen | Evaluator |
| Don Radford | |
| Roy Richards | |
| Mary Horn | |

Made and printed by Waterlow (Dunstable) Limited

# General preface

'Science 5/13' is a project sponsored jointly by the Schools Council, the Nuffield Foundation and the Scottish Education Department, and based at the University of Bristol School of Education. It aims at helping teachers to help children between the ages of five and thirteen years to learn science through first-hand experience using a variety of methods.

The Project produces books that comprise Units dealing with subject-areas in which children are likely to conduct investigations. Some of these Units are supported by books of background information. The Units are linked by objectives that the Project team hopes children will attain through their work. The aims of the Project are explained in a general guide for teachers called *With objectives in mind,* which contains the Project's guide to Objectives for children learning science, reprinted at the back of each Unit.

## Acknowledgements

The Project is deeply grateful to its many friends: to the local education authorities who have helped us work in their areas, to those of their staff who, acting as area representatives, have borne the heavy brunt of administering our trials, and to the teachers, heads and wardens who have been generous without stint in working with their children on our materials. The books we have written drew substance from the work they did for us, and it was through their critical appraisal that our materials reached their present form. For guidance, we had our sponsors, our Consultative Committee and, for support, in all our working, the University of Bristol. To all of them we acknowledge our many debts: their help has been invaluable.

In the production of this book we gratefully acknowledge the assistance of the following organisations:

Timber Research and Development Association
Forestry Commission
Forest Research Products
The Timber Trade Federation of the United Kingdom.

## Metrication

This has given us a great deal to think about. We have been given much good advice by well-informed friends, and we have consulted many reports by learned bodies. Following the advice and the reports wherever possible we have expressed quantities in metric units with Imperial units afterwards in square brackets if it seemed useful to state them so.

There are, however, some cases to which the recommendations are difficult to apply. For instance we have difficulty with units such as miles per hour (which has statutory force in this country) and with some Imperial units that are still in current use for common commodities and, as far as we know, liable to remain so for some time. In these cases we have tried to use our common sense, and, in order to make statements that are both accurate and helpful to teachers we have quoted Imperial measures followed by the approximate metric equivalent in square brackets if it seemed sensible to give them.

Where we have quoted statements made by children, or given illustrations that are children's work, we have left unaltered the units in which the children worked—in any case some of these units were arbitrary.

# Contents

# Introduction

'People who spend their lives working with timber become emotionally attached to it. There is also an intellectual fascination in the paradoxes it presents; particularly now, when unexpected truths about its nature are shown in more contrasting light cast by rigorous technology. Although it burns, it is found to provide excellent fire resistance. Although it is light, walls and floors can be built with it to give excellent sound insulation. Although it is the oldest of structural materials and went out of fashion amongst engineers long ago during the Industrial Revolution, it has now become a front runner in the industrialised building field. As men become obsessed with synthesising new building plastics to meet new performance standards as to strength, stiffness, specific weight, thermal conductivity, specific heat, thermal expansion, fire resistance, permeability, durability, disposability, workability, texture, colour, aesthetic quality, low productional cost, etc., etc., we find, by searching Nature's catalogue of trees, that most of what we seek is here, given the knowledge to use it properly.'

W. Ollis (taken from the *Construction Industries Handbook*.)

Here in a nutshell is the fascination of wood. It has emotional and intellectual appeal for those who work closely with it. Direct contact with the material develops its emotional appeal; intellectual appeal grows from knowing more about it. And the more one learns about wood the more its emotional appeal increases; it is an immensely satisfying material to work with and to think about.

This book is written for teachers who wish to gain more knowledge of wood. It is presented as a source of factual information that complements the classroom activities suggested in *Working with wood, Stages 1 & 2*. It is not a book for children. Much of the material it contains is too detailed or too abstract for their understanding, but we hope it will benefit them indirectly when teacher and children investigate wood together.

# 1 The nature of wood

Scots pine timber

We can put wood into certain categories on the basis of our general experience with materials. We might describe it in terms of weight—*is it heavy or light?* and of feel—*is it warm or cold, rough or smooth?* And we might comment on its smell.

We can also link its appearance to our wider experience of wood. Is it a common wood? Have we seen it used in furniture or for common household articles? How does it compare with other woods in our surroundings?

Such observations yield immediate information and may promote further questions:

What kind of tree does the wood come from?
Does the tree grow locally?
Which part of the tree does it come from?
How does a tree make wood?
How is wood made ready for use?
What is it used for?
Why is it used for particular things?
What is wood like inside?

The answer to questions of this kind cannot come from handling wood in a general way; they require information or more specialised experience. All the questions are relevant to understanding the nature of wood but the last is probably most fundamental, since some appreciation of what wood is like inside is essential in order to put factual information about the material in the right perspective.

The picture opposite shows what part of the timber surface looks like when it is magnified ten times.

We can discover quite a lot about a piece of wood from direct observation:

We can notice its colour and markings and comment on its texture. These are not the same all over, since careful looking reveals that the patterns we see depend on how the wood has been sawn.

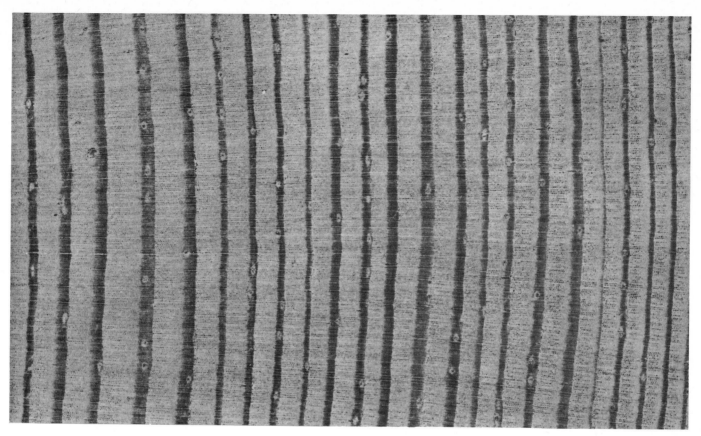

Wood magnified approximately ten times

With unaided eyes we see the surface as a comparatively uniform structure of light and dark bands, but magnification shows clearly that each band is far from uniform. We can now discriminate certain well-defined structures and notice lines and holes that were not previously visible. In other words we can begin to appreciate its structural differentiation. This is an important observation because the nature of wood—its appearance and properties—relates directly to the kind, number and arrangements of the various component parts inside it.

Let us now look at wood magnified 400 times as shown in the photograph on page 4.

Here the structural differentiation is more marked and even greater detail emerges. Without specialised knowledge we cannot name or account for it, but we can appreciate that we are looking at a highly organised material.

Finally let us look at the photograph on page 5. This is a picture of wood recorded by an electron microscope with a magnification of about 4000.

It's difficult from this photograph for the non-specialist to class the material as wood; it looks more like clay. But it is wood and we are looking at part of the intricate structure of a pit in

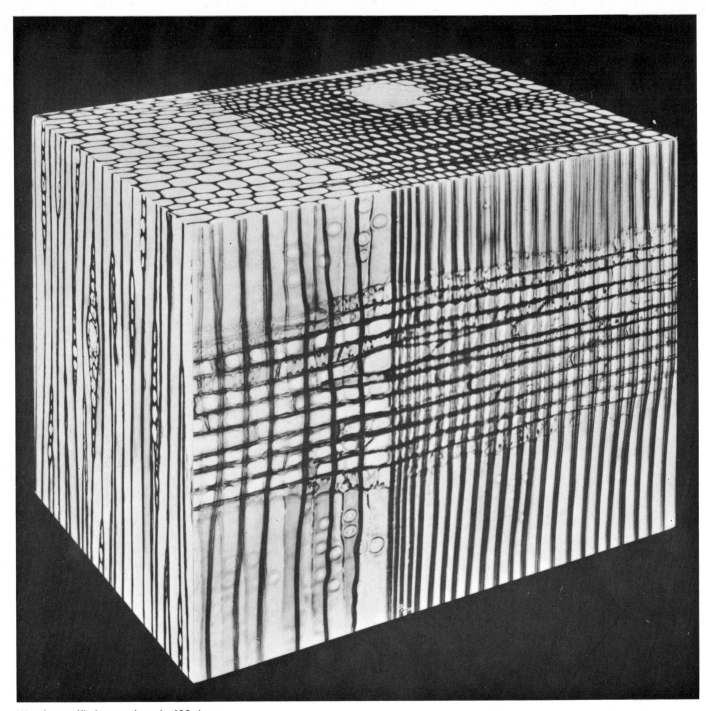

Wood magnified approximately 400 times

4

the wall of a spruce wood cell. At this level of magnification wood makes a strong impression. Some people key in to its visual appeal, seeing it as a source of creative work : others are amazed at the degree of complexity that exists in something so commonplace. Clearly there is more to wood than meets the eye.

Wood is a complex, highly organised material. Any piece has certain features of construction that are found in all woods, but at the same time it is unique. It is just not possible to get two pieces of wood that are identical in every way ; this is the fascination of the material and its challenge for man. We can amass information about it, generalise about its properties and make broad statements about its use ; but, underlying all the hard facts of succeeding chapters, we should keep in mind an appreciation that wood is infinitely varied and variable in nature.

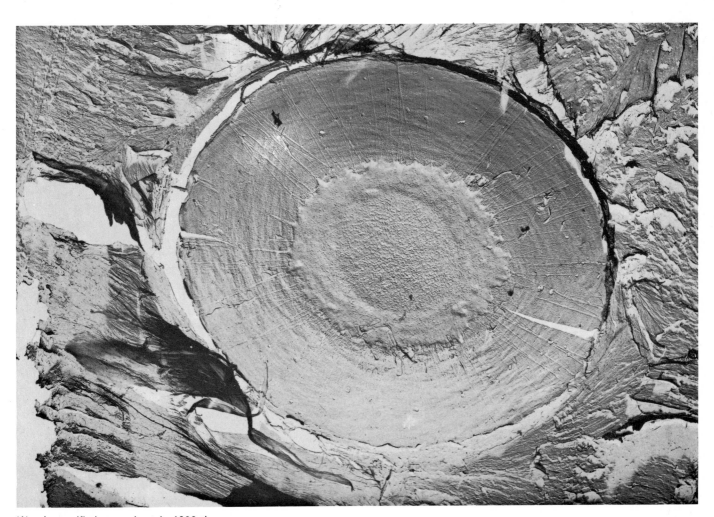

Wood magnified approximately 4000 times

# 2 Timber from trees

## 2.1 How a tree makes wood

It is a staggering thought that a tiny acorn weighing so little can grow into a tree which in its lifetime may produce many cubic metres of wood. When we consider that the raw materials used to make the wood are all comparatively simple substances absorbed from the surroundings, this is a tremendous feat of productivity by any standards.

Wood is produced as a tree grows, and the growth of trees, like the growth of any living thing, is a fascinating and complex process. It is, however, outside the scope of this book. We are concerned here, not with fine detail, but with the general pattern of a tree's growth in relation to the wood it forms. In other words, we are looking at a tree as a timber-manufacturing unit.

Every manufacturing site requires raw materials, and a tree is no exception. It takes in water from the soil, carbon dioxide from the air and, in its leaves with the aid of energy derived from sunlight, new materials are built up. What happens to these new materials is a complicated story involving much chemical activity in many parts of the tree. The first formed materials are broken down and the resultant 'bits' are involved in a variety of processes : some becoming associated with other raw materials which the tree absorbs from the soil.

It is not possible in a few sentences to explain the numerous chemical actions that occur in a tree before a molecule of wood is produced. Sufficient perhaps in our concern with the production of timber, to know that the particular material we call wood is made in certain parts of the tree, but that its manufacture is dependent on incredibly intricate activity involving the whole tree.

All wood is produced by the living cells of the *cambium*. This layer of cells, a mere 0·25 mm in thickness, is responsible for the production of a tree trunk which may exceed a metre in diameter. It is clearly an important component in the manufacture of wood and as such warrants attention. Its position relative to the other parts of a tree trunk is shown in this diagram.

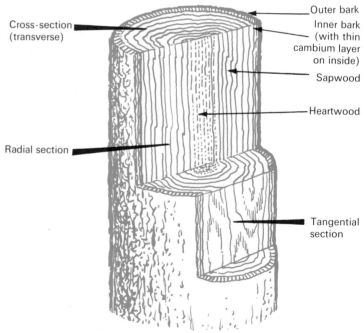

Cross-section (transverse)

Radial section

Outer bark

Inner bark (with thin cambium layer on inside)

Sapwood

Heartwood

Tangential section

The structure of a tree trunk

If we are to understand the contribution made by the cambium in the production of wood, it is helpful to first comment on the other layers shown in the diagram opposite.

The *outer bark* is the tree's protection from the outside world. It keeps out water, insulates against cold and heat, guards against pests and diseases and prevents loss of water from the internal layers.

Beneath the outer bark there is a region of special cells called the *phloem* layer—it may also be referred to as inner bark, or bast. The phloem can be thought of as a 'pipeline' through which food is passed round the tree. It lives for only a short time and then dies, turns to cork and becomes part of the protective bark. New phloem is produced by the outer side of the cambium layer which also produces new cells on its inner side.

The cells produced internally to the cambium make up the *sapwood* and the layer they form can also be thought of as a 'pipeline', but one through which water moves up to the leaves—an activity which is greatest in spring when the sap rises. Sapwood is new wood.

As more sapwood is formed by the cambium, the inner cells of the existing sapwood die and turn to *heartwood*. Heartwood forms the central supporting pillar of the tree : its cells, although dead, are enormously strong.

A tree trunk then is a well-organised structure, made up of different layers. The innermost layers, the heartwood and sapwood, are the layers which man uses as timber. They make up the main bulk of a tree trunk but it is as well to remember that all the vast amount of timber we have around us originated from the cambium layer in the tree trunk—a layer which is structurally insignificant but vitally important.

Cambium cells completely encircle a tree—they are present in its trunk, branches and twigs—and, providing the conditions of the environment are favourable to growth, they are constantly producing new wood on their inner surface. As a result, the tree increases in girth and the cambium continually moves outwards, leaving the weight-supporting wood behind it. In our climate, growth is seasonal and wood is formed in a series of annual or growth rings which make it possible to tell the age of any stem which has been cut across. New wood is produced in spring and summer (none being formed in autumn and winter) and differences in the amount and nature of the cells of the new tissue give spring and summer wood a different appearance. These differences show themselves as the annual rings : one ring of spring wood and one ring of summer wood represent one year's growth.

Growth resulting in increase in the height of a tree and hence the amount of timber it can produce, occurs only at the extreme end of the trunk and branches. Once the tree's characteristic branching is complete no further appreciable increase in height normally occurs, although increase in girth may take place throughout its entire life. The increase in girth is, as we have seen, the result of the activity of the cells of the cambium layer, and to complete our appreciation of the manufacture of wood by a tree it may be helpful to extend our awareness of the internal structure of the trunk.

We have built up a picture of wood being laid down in organised layers. This is perfectly true, but it is important to realise that the layers of wood have themselves an organised structure ; that each layer is not made up of one kind of cell only. Different kinds of cell occur in this woody tissue and the differences in their structure can be related to differences in the work they do. Detailed explanation of the differences is not relevant here, but it is perhaps of value to realise that new cells produced by the cambium undergo changes as they develop and age : they give rise to different kinds of cells. It is the kind and arrangement of the cells within woody tissue that gives wood its particular appearance and properties.

Growth rings of an oak tree. How old is the tree?

## 2.2 Hardwood and softwood

To the average person all wood is wood, but where wood is used commercially it is customary to distinguish between hardwood and softwood. Hardwood comes from hardwood trees and softwood from softwood trees. This may seem an obvious statement, but it is a helpful one since the distinction is based on the features of the tree from which timber is obtained, and bears no relationship to the relative hardness or softness of the wood itself. For example, balsa is a very soft wood produced by a hardwood tree : yew is a hard wood produced by a softwood tree.

Softwood and hardwood trees can easily be distinguished by the shape of their leaves. All hardwood trees, such as oak, ash, elm, have broad leaves ; the leaves of softwood trees, pine, larch, yew, for instance, are needle or scale-like. It is not quite as easy to distinguish between softwood and hardwood timber as it is to recognise the trees, but the task presents little difficulty if the wood is examined in a particular way :

a. Locate the transverse or end section (see 2.1) (a clean even cut across the section with a sharp blade will make examination easier, as torn cell ends will give a false impression).
b. Examine the end section for the presence of small holes. (For many timbers the unaided eye can detect these holes, but it is helpful to use a hand lens ( × 10).)
c. If, on examination, holes can be seen, the wood is a *hardwood*.
d. If no holes are visible the wood is very probably a *softwood*.

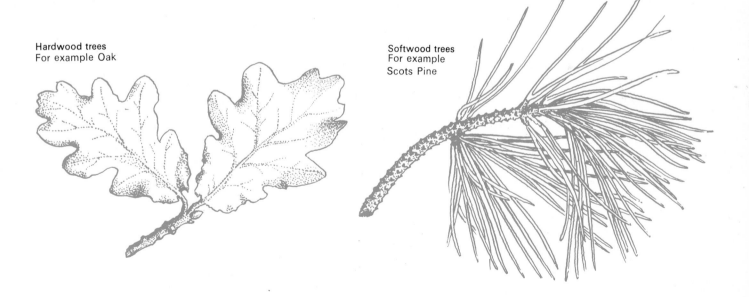

Hardwood trees
For example Oak

Softwood trees
For example
Scots Pine

Hardwood trees, eg oak, have broad leaves.
Most are deciduous but some are evergreen eg holly.
They produce hardwood timber which is usually hard but may be soft.

Softwood trees, eg Scots pine have needle-like leaves.
Practically all are evergreen but some shed their leaves eg larch.
They produce softwood timber which is usually soft but may be hard.

This immediate and simple identification is applicable to all commercial timbers. It is based on the fact that hardwood contains some special cells called *vessels* have characteristically large cavities : vessels do not occur in softwoods.

The identification of unknown individual hardwoods and softwoods is a specialist task that requires technical knowledge and experience.

## 2.3 Preparing wood for use

### Tree felling
The techniques used depend on where a tree grows but the general considerations are how to fell the tree :

a. with safety (for workers and perhaps surrounding structures and other trees),

b. as economically as possible.

Trees grouped in forests present peculiar problems and the type of felling largely depends on the number and distribution of trees that have commercial importance. Where trees grow close together and all have commercial value (eg Canadian lumber forests), all trees over a large area are felled, but large-scale felling is not used in forests where only a few of the numerous trees

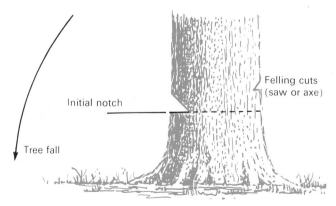

The position of the original notch determines which way the tree will fall

have commercial value (eg tropical rain forests where only approximately ten percent have value).

Trees are commonly felled by making an initial wedge-shaped cut on one side of the trunk, then cutting through the trunk from the other side so that the tree falls away from the felling cuts.

Very large trees with extended or buttress bases are often cut off several metres from the ground, thus saving work and labour in transporting uncommercial timber. In order to do this men making the initial notch are supported in some way.

## Logging
This is the term given to all the different jobs required to get a tree from the place where it was cut to a saw-mill. It involves:

a. trimming the felled tree and possibly cutting the trunk into smaller logs,

b. transporting logs.

The techniques used depend on the scale of felling and the availability of mechanised transport. Wherever possible, rivers are used for long-distance transport (economical) and the logs are carried down loose or formed into rafts (some tropical hardwoods are so dense that they do not float and these 'sinkers' are lashed to lighter logs that float easily). Where no suitable rivers exist transport will be overland by rail or road. In areas of large-scale felling sophisticated methods of transport may be found, such as the use of overhead hoists. In other situations logs may be hauled by gangs of men, teams of oxen, or, as in Burma, by trained elephants.

## Sawing ('conversion') of timber
This is a highly skilled occupation by which the required kind of timber is obtained from a log.

Logs ready for transit in British Columbia. Notice the size of the lumbermen, look at the logs. See how closely the trees grow together. What would be a rough estimate of the volume of timber harvested from the felled area?

Power saw at work in Kaingaroa forest in New Zealand. Trees are felled here at the rate of one a minute.

Quarter-sawn

Flat-sawn (also called plain or slash-sawn)

Planks cut radially

Planks cut tangentially

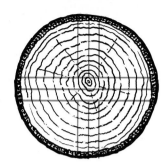

Radially sawn timber is more expensive because more handling is required but the wood warps less and often shows better figuring

Flat-sawn timber is cheaper but the planks are liable to warp

Various saws and techniques for sawing exist but the use of a particular saw and the method of cutting depends on the nature of the unsawn log and the kind of sections required.

The trees may be sawn to obtain the maximum amount of usable timber, or they may be cut a certain way in order to obtain maximum strength from the wood or to give the wood a particular attractive appearance.

In practice a log is normally either *flat-sawn* or *quarter-sawn*. To understand these terms it is necessary to refer to 2.1.

Flat-sawn wood is obtained when a log is cut tangentially ; quarter-sawn wood is obtained by radial cutting.

After the various sawing procedures have taken place, the planks of timber are stacked for seasoning. Afterwards they may be sold as rough-sawn wood or as prepared or dressed wood (dressed wood has been through a planing machine).

## Seasoning
Seasoning is the removal of moisture from wood. As a result of seasoning, timber is dried to a certain moisture content. (This term is defined in Section 4.2.)

Correctly seasoned timber is :

More resistant to decay.

Less likely to shrink and warp and so has greater stability in use.
Stronger.
Lighter in weight and so easier to handle.
Easier to work and finish.
Easier to treat with paint, varnish and wood preservatives.

Most wooden objects are made from seasoned timber, but for some activities, such as turning and clogmaking, 'green' timber is used.

There are two chief methods of seasoning :

a. *Air* (*natural*) *seasoning*. Timber is stacked in the open, in such a way that :

There is an even regulated air circulation around the planks so that moisture in the wood can evaporate away.

The stack of wood is protected from rain and sun, and from contact with the ground.

The exposed ends of timber are protected in some way to prevent splitting.

A sample plank can be easily withdrawn from the stack so that the seasoning process can be checked.

In this manner the timber dries gradually (25-mm planks of beech may require about eight months) but the actual time needed for the required seasoning depends on the kind of timber, the thickness of the planks and atmospheric conditions of wind speed, temperature and humidity.

Air seasoning gives a minimum moisture content of eighteen percent (4.2).

b. *Kiln (forced) seasoning*. Kiln seasoning was introduced at the beginning of this century and research into the process received great impetus towards the end of World War I. The method is used when it is necessary to season timber more quickly, or to obtain a lower moisture content than can be obtained in the open air. The timber is dried more quickly in a kiln under carefully controlled conditions of moisture and heat—lack of control may cause serious shrinking and warping and a whole load of expensive timber may be rendered useless.

Here is an example of a kiln seasoning process :

The wood is put in contact with low heat and considerable steam which enables it to retain its moisture, thus preventing splitting from too quick drying.

The heat is then increased and the steam decreased in order that the wood will lose water without splitting.

The wood is finally heated to a higher temperature in contact with less steam.

During the whole process the airflow over the wood is carefully regulated and in this manner its drying can be controlled.

The time required for kiln seasoning of wood varies with the kind of wood used, its thickness and the efficiency of the kilning process : 25-mm beech can be dried from twenty-two per cent mc (see 4.2.) to ten per cent mc in five days ; 38-mm beech dried to the same mc requires eight days.

Using kiln processing, wood may be dried to as little as four per cent mc. Such a low moisture content could never be achieved by air drying.

14

# 3 Sources of timber

Timber is one of the few replaceable raw materials available to man and, although wood is being superseded by new materials such as plastics for many traditional uses, it is likely that we will always require vast quantities of timber for use both in its natural state and for processing to make other things.

## 3.1 World sources

On a world scale, the available timber resources are, as yet, adequate for all needs, but as a nation we are unable to produce anything approaching the amount of timber we consume daily. Great Britain imports more timber and timber products than any other country in the world and this has considerable economic and social implications. British timber sources are drawn from every major forest belt in the world.

From the map of the world distribution of natural vegetation shown on page 17, we can see that the land areas of the world are forested in broad belts.

Each belt is associated with a particular kind of environment having climatic conditions which favour the growth of certain trees. Where the climate is hostile to growth as, for example, in the polar regions, no trees grow. This is an over-simplified generalisation : the distribution of trees is, of course, not as clearcut as the diagram suggests. For example, Iceland is shown to be in a treeless belt yet the island has a number of trees, albeit chiefly dwarf varieties. Further, there are places in the tropical hardwood belt where other kinds of tree grow. In mountainous regions of the tropics, tree zonation may be encountered that is associated with different altitudes, as, for example, on Mount Kenya.

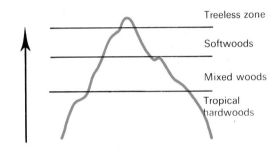

Tree zonation as seen in mountainous tropical areas

Detailed explanation of forest distribution is not relevant in a general appreciation of timber; it is sufficient to appreciate that there is a pattern in the distribution of trees and that this pattern has a bearing on man's activity in relation to timber. It influences any tree planting he may undertake and has an important effect on world trade.

## 3.2 British timber imports

In Great Britain the proportion of available land devoted to the raising of tree crops is little more than seven per cent, among the lowest in Europe. It is not, therefore, surprising that our supplies of home-grown timber are completely inadequate for our requirements and as a result we have to import vast quantities of wood. Indeed, ninety percent of all wood used in Great Britain

A tree nursery with forestry technician trainees, in the Amazon area of Peru

16

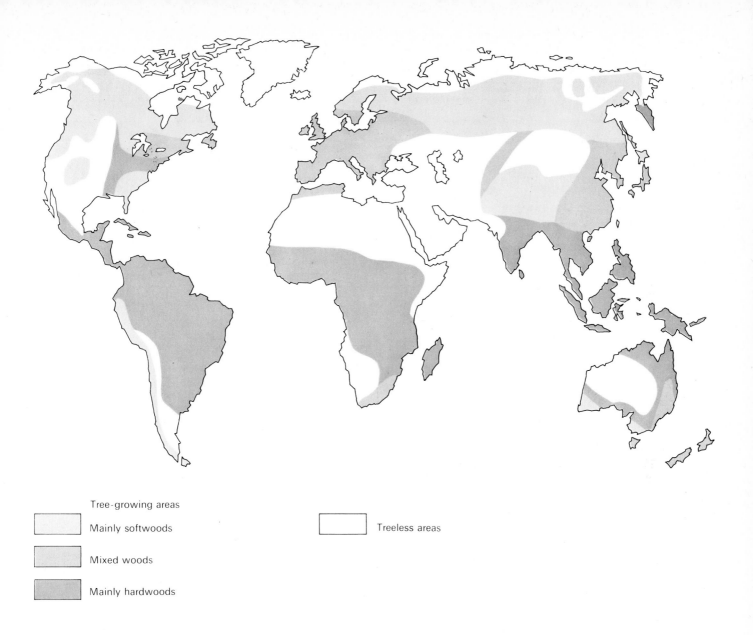

Tree-growing areas

Mainly softwoods

Mixed woods

Mainly hardwoods

Treeless areas

These vegetational belts give some indication of the timber-producing areas of the world

| Journey of Timber | Some People Involved |
|---|---|

TIMBER IS OBTAINED FROM TREES GROWING OVERSEAS → Overseas shipper who usually owns the timber

→ Workers concerned with felling, logging, sawing, grading and clerical tasks

TIMBER IS TRANSPORTED BY SEA → Overseas representatives of British timber agents

→ Workers concerned with loading and shipping

TIMBER ENTERS BRITAIN → Timber agents' salesmen

→ British timber importers

TIMBER IS STORED IN BULK → Workers involved in storing and selling operations

TIMBER IS SOLD → Workers concerned with transport, resawing and clerical procedures.

To timber merchants for resale, e g builders, carpenters, cabinet makers, 'Do-It-Yourself' Shops

To large firms for direct use, e g furniture making, construction work

Note: Advisory specialists may be involved at all stages.

18

is grown in other countries: in 1969 this amounted to some 9 million cubic metres, which represents an import bill of over £200 million.

Clearly such a dependence upon imported timber has far-reaching effects on a community. It necessitates 'high-level 'consideration of economic implications and requires complex organisation to deal with the practicalities of timber buying, transportation and distribution. The number of people whose work involves them with aspects of timber importing might well surprise us. Take for example the people involved when a shipment of timber arrives at a British port for distribution and use inland. We might represent some of the people involved in such a journey as shown in the diagram.

London, Hull, Liverpool, Avonmouth, Manchester and Glasgow are the main ports through which foreign timber enters Great Britain. The following tables show the chief timbers imported to the UK.

Imported timber usually bears a *shipper's mark*, which is painted or branded on the end of a plank. A shipper's mark is really a trademark. Each shipper has a selection of marks covering the quality of timber he produces and he takes care to maintain the standards they represent. It is the job of the importer to note these standards and assess the value of one shipper's mark in relation to others.

A layman noticing such marks would pay little attention to them, but to the expert they represent a coded form of information. Each mark when it is 'read' gives details of such things as the shipper, the country of origin of the timber, the port through which it was shipped and the nature and quality of the timber. Thus the mark 'KS' informs an importer that the timber was shipped by A/S Kjoita Sagbruk and Hövleri, through a port Kristiansand in Norway, and that the shipper exports unsorted planed and sawn redwood and whitewood.

There are thousands of such marks; the principal ones, and their explanations, can be found in the

## Chief imported hardwoods

| Name of timber | Main source | Chief use |
|---|---|---|
| Teak | Burma | Very high-class joinery |
| Iroko | West Africa | Substitute for teak |
| African mahogany | West Africa | General joinery |
| Sapele | West Africa | General joinery Flooring |
| Utile | West Africa | General joinery Flooring |
| Keruing | South-east Asia | Door and window sills Flooring |
| Afrormosia | West Africa | Doors High-class joinery |
| Abura | West Africa | Mouldings * Joinery High-class joinery |
| Obeche | West Africa | Interior cabinet work |
| Ramin | Malaya | Mouldings* Joinery |
| Oak | Japan/America | High-class joinery Flooring |
| Beech | Europe (chiefly Rumania and Czechoslovakia) | Furniture |

\* Moulding is a general term which covers such things as skirting boards, architraves and picture rails.

## Chief imported softwoods

| Name of timber | Main source | Chief use |
|---|---|---|
| Hemlock | Canada/USA | General Carcassing * |
| Douglas fir | Canada/USA | General Carcassing * |
| Western red cedar | Canada | External Cladding † Shingles ‡ |
| Spruce | Canada/ Scandinavia | Carcassing * Planks |
| European redwood | Scandinavia | Carcassing * General joinery |
| Parana pine | Brazil | High-class joinery |

\* Carcassing refers to the general structural timbers of buildings.
† Cladding refers to external boarding of sheds and houses.
‡ Shingles refers to natural timber roofing tiles.

*Timber Year Book and Diary,* published by Lomax, Erskine Publications Ltd.

Some examples of shipping marks are shown below, together with the port from which the timber is shipped.

**A·U·B**  Oslo, Norway

**ALBE**  Gothenburg, Sweden

**H·S·K**  Hamina, Finland

**NH**  Vancouver, Canada

  Tokyo, Japan

  Singapore, Malaysia

  Takoradi, Ghana

Calabar, Nigeria

Gulf of Mexico ports, USA

Shipping marks identify the quality of the wood as well as its port of shipment

### 3.3 Home-grown timber

Home-grown timber, as we have seen, accounts for under ten percent of our total consumption of wood and the forest policy of Great Britain is directed to redressing this unfavourable situation. The Forestry Commission is responsible for large-scale replanting and forestation schemes and, in addition, the Commission gives advice to private landowners who may receive financial assistance from the Government for woodland management. As part of this plan the vast majority of trees now planted in Britain are softwood species, since these, largely by virtue of their quicker growth, give better economic return than do hardwoods. Consequently, the pattern of tree cover in Britain is undergoing a change, and it is probable that in a century or so from now broad-leaved trees will be very scarce, at least in woodland managed for commercial purposes.

The policy of restocking and extending our forests necessitates considerable research into the kinds of tree which are best suited to our climate, which will thrive with the minimum of care and produce timber suited to commercial requirements. As a consequence, trees which are not normally native to Britain have been introduced into our forests and it is likely that this process will continue, for the Forestry Commission's commitment to research and development in this area is, and must be, a continuous one.

The list opposite sets out our home-grown timbers of economic significance, but it does not indicate the relative importance of each individual species.

## Hardwoods

| Major species | Minor species |
| --- | --- |
| Alder | Apple |
| Ash | Cherry |
| Beech | Holly |
| Birch | Hornbeam |
| Chestnut | Maples |
| Elm | Lime |
| Oak | Walnut |
| Poplar | Willow |
| Sycamore | |

## Softwoods

| Major species | Minor species |
| --- | --- |
| Douglas fir | Silver fir |
| Larch : | Western hemlock |
| European Japanese Hybrid | Western red cedar |
| Pine : | |
| Scots Corsican Lodgepole | |
| Spruce : | |
| Norway Sitka | |

# 4 Properties of timber

The properties of timber may conveniently be divided into :

*Visual properties.* These, in general, relate to man's aesthetic use of timber and include such things as colour, pattern (figuring), smell. Such properties relate to the kind, arrangement and composition of the cells of timber and the way it has been prepared for use. They are not generally measurable.

*Functional properties.* These relate to the functional use of timber and include such things as mechanical properties and behaviour with respect to water, heat, etc. Such properties also depend on the kind and arrangement of the cells in the wood—that is, on its cellular structure. These properties can be measured—indeed, they need to be for the safe and efficient use of wood as a material.

In this section we shall be concerned with functional properties of timber.

## 4.1 The structure of wood cells (as an aid to understanding the functional properties of timber)

Timber is largely composed of numerous tubular cells which fit closely together rather like a bundle of drinking straws with their ends overlapping. These cells, like the cells of all plants, have their walls chiefly composed of the chemical substance *cellulose* (but other substances are also present, eg *lignin*). Cellulose is a 'long-chain molecule' that is to say, it is made up of a number of sub-units joined together in a particular way

which we might represent as shown below.

The basic unit of cellulose is glucose, and a cellulose chain may contain several hundred glucose units. Chemical detail need not concern us here, merely the general idea that the long cells of wood have walls made up of linear structures lying parallel to the length of the cell.

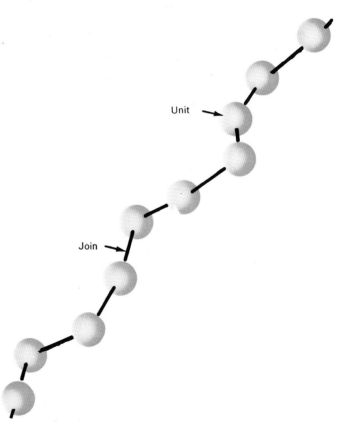

Unit →

Join →

The cellulose molecule has a long chain-like structure

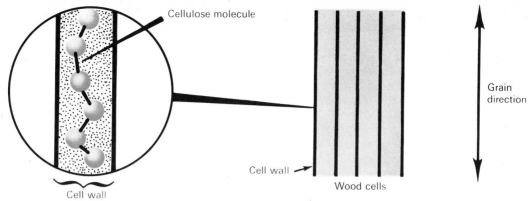

The molecules are aligned with the cell walls, and wood is strongest along the grain

This arrangement has an important bearing on the mechanical properties of timber which will be described later (4.3).

Timbers differ in the thickness of their cell walls, ie the amount of wood substance present. This variation accounts for differences in the density of different woods, and hence for certain differences in properties.

The density of wood is expressed in kilogrammes per cubic metre. Seasoned balsa has a density of about 80–60 kg/m³ whilst the density of seasoned oak is about 730–760 kg/m³.

It is important to realise that different woods, although they conform to the same general pattern, vary considerably in structure and hence in properties. Wood is a natural material and shows considerable variation. There are many different kinds of timbers and, in addition, timber from different trees of the same species may vary a great deal—indeed, no two pieces of wood from the *same* tree are identical. Such variation makes it far more difficult to specify exactly the functional properties of any one piece of timber, than it is to specify, for example, the properties of a piece of steel.

When man uses wood he must make allowances for all possible variation that may exist in its properties.

## 4.2 Wood and water

The woody material of a standing tree is almost completely saturated with water, yet timber is required for use in an almost dry state.

Many of the problems associated with the preparation and use of wood can be related to its water content. Water in wood is a nuisance because :

a. Wet wood weighs more and this puts up handling and transport costs.

b. Wet wood has only about one-third of the stiffness of dry wood.

c. Changes in the water content of wood cause shrinkage and swelling and hence movement of wood in use.

d. Water in wood encourages attack from insects and fungi.

For these reasons it is important to know the amount of water present in wood samples.

The amount of water present in a piece of timber is referred to as its *moisture content* (mc) and is usually expressed as a percentage of the dry weight of the wood, ie

$$mc = \frac{\text{initial weight} - \text{dry weight}}{\text{weight of dry wood}} \times 100\%.$$

When wood is seasoned it is dried to the particular moisture content required, but this drying is not necessarily permanent, since wood behaves in a peculiar way with respect to moisture. It will take up or lose moisture depending on the atmospheric conditions of its surroundings.

Dry wood in damp surroundings will absorb water and swell. Wet wood in dry surroundings will lose moisture and possibly shrink. This property of wood is very important in considering man's use of the material. Different timbers vary in the amount of water they lose or take up, but all are hygroscopic—ie they lose or gain water until their water content is the same as (in equilibrium with) that of their surroundings.

To appreciate the hygroscopic nature of timber it is helpful to consider the location of water in woody material. Water occurs in the cell cavities of wood cells ('free' water) and also in the cell walls themselves (here it is combined with materials of the wall and is known as 'bound' water).

When a piece of wood is at its maximum moisture content, there is water in both the cell cavities and the cell walls, but, as the wood dries, the 'free' water from the cell cavities is gradually lost until at about thirty percent mc the only water present in the wood is the 'bound' water of the cell walls. Drying beyond this point results in the removal of 'bound' water molecules from the wall which as a result is reduced in size. The effect of this throughout all the cells in a piece of wood is to cause an appreciable shrinkage of the timber.

Should dry wood (ie wood below thirty percent mc) come in contact with moisture, water will enter and unite with the cell wall material causing it to swell. When the walls have taken up as much 'bound' water as they can, no more swelling occurs and any further water entering the wood is held as 'free' water in the cell cavities.

Many changes are observable in the dimensions of wood in use, as a result of its hygroscopic properties. Doors, gates and wooden window frames may become tight in their frames during the damp winter months, yet easy to open after a dry spell. Furniture and structural timbers are likely to shrink and possibly crack when central heating is newly installed in an old house, and many of the plaster cracks appearing in new houses can be traced to shrinkage of constructural wood as the house dries out. The 'ghost noises' of old houses are most often caused by wood moving as a result of a night-time drop in temperature and a consequent alteration in the amount of water vapour held in the air.

Wood does not 'move' equally in all directions; shrinkage 'along the grain', ie in length, is negligible compared with 'across the grain' shrinkage (this is related to the chain molecule structure of cellulose). For example, a plank of

**Wood undergoes changes as it gains or loses water**

| Water content of wood cells | Water content of cell wall | Water content of cell cavity |
|---|---|---|
| Saturated with water | Saturated with 'bound' water | Full of water |
| *Further contact with water* ↕ *Drying* | | |
| At about 30% m.c. | Saturated | Empty |
| *Contact with water* ↕ *Further drying* | | |
| At less than 30% m.c. | Shrinks by loss of 'bound' water | Empty |

| Moisture content (%) | Appropriate use | Correct seasoning |
|---|---|---|
| 27 | *Appreciable shrinkage starts* | |
| 26 | Maximum for rough carpentry | |
| 25 | | |
| 24 | | |
| 23 | | |
| 22 | | Can be |
| 21 | | obtained |
| 20 | Maximum for general carpentry | by air drying |
| | *Dry rot safety line* (ie dry rot unlikely when moisture content is less than this) | |
| 19 | | |
| 18 | External joinery | |
| 17 ) | External doors, agricultural | |
| 16 ) | implements, garden furniture | |
| 15 | Wood used in aircraft, cars, ship's decks | |
| 14 ) | Bedroom furniture and wood in slightly or occasionally heated | |
| 13 ) | buildings | |
| 12 | Wood in continuously heated buildings | Kiln seasoning is necessary |
| 11 | | |
| 10 | Wood in situations with high degree of central heating, eg hospitals, offices | |
| 9 | | |
| 8 | Wood flooring over heating elements | |

wood 250 mm wide may shrink by as much as 25 mm in width, but show no measurable decrease in length. Such differential shrinkage must be allowed for in wood used for construction work.

Some timbers, teak for instance, are remarkably stable in use ; others fluctuate widely with changing atmospheric conditions. To prevent excessive movement, timber should be dried to a moisture content applicable to its conditions of use.

Suitable moisture contents of timber for various purposes are indicated in the table above.

There can be little doubt that the amount of moisture in timber is an important consideration in everyday life, and a reliable means of preventing the entry of water into carefully seasoned wood is commercially desirable. However, at the moment there is no way of completely preventing the intake of water by wood. It is possible in some situations to apply water barriers, such as creosote, but the slightest crack in the barrier will permit the entry of moisture. Various 'waterproofing' materials exist but it is not possible at present to adequately waterproof wood. All surface treatments, such as oiling, painting and varnishing, merely delay the uptake of water; they do not in themselves decrease the ability of the cell walls to absorb water.

## 4.3 Mechanical properties

The 'man in the street' is unlikely to have much understanding of the mechanical properties of timber. He takes it for granted that his roof will stay up, that he will not normally fall through the floor boards, that he can walk across a wooden bridge with safety. He may on occasion talk about the strength of wood in relation to the breaking and bending of wooden things about him, or perhaps refer to the hardness of wooden objects; but he seldom thinks, nor indeed needs to think, about the effect the mechanical properties of wood have on its use.

The mechanical properties of timber relate to the way it behaves when subjected to applied forces. Such forces may act externally on the wood or internally: they are termed stresses.

Three kinds of stresses can affect timber:

a. *Compression* stresses: tend to crush timber.

b. *Tensile* stresses: tend to elongate timber.

c. *Shear* stresses: tend to cause one portion of a piece of wood to slide over another.

When we notice wood bending, we are really observing the changes occurring in wood as a result of a combination of all three stresses.

Wood varies in its resistance to stress, in other words, it varies in *strength* (the strength of timber is the resistance it has to stress). For any constructional work involving wood it is vital to know how a particular kind of wood reacts to compression, tension and shear forces, ie to appreciate its compression, tensile and shear strength.

The strength of timber is related to:

a. *The kind of timber.* In general, the denser the wood, the stronger it is.

b. *The amount of moisture present in the wood.* Dry wood is stronger than wet wood.

c. *The direction of the grain.* Timber has greater compression and tensile strength along the grain than across the grain, but greater shear strength across the grain. This is to be expected from the structure of wood. A piece of wood is really a bundle of tubes joined together and the influence of grain direction is best appreciated by exploring the strength of a bundle of drinking straws.

Generally, it is much easier to crush wood by compression *across* the grain rather than with the grain. This is also true for tensile stress. On the other hand it is easier to shear wood *with* the grain rather than across it. It is interesting to note that the main stress in a standing tree is a compression stress resulting from the weight of the branches and foliage, and that in a tree the grain runs vertically, ie the stress is acting with the grain. As a result of the compression stress the timber in a tree is densest at its base.

Stresses acting on wood tend to cause a change in shape and size and this distortion is known as a strain.

The amount of strain (deformation) occurring in timber is proportional to the stress acting upon it. The greater the stress, the greater the deformation. If the stress causing a strain is small, and is acting upon the wood for a short time, then the amount of deformation of the wood is said to be recoverable, ie the wood can return to its original shape and size—it has elastic properties. If, however, the stress increases, a point is reached beyond which further stress causes a permanent change in the wood which eventually ruptures

The largest timber dome structure in the United Kingdom. Its construction required skilled knowledge and application of the mechanical properties of wood

and breaks. This is known as the limit of elasticity. In this respect wood behaves like many other materials.

The amount of non-recoverable strain which a wood can absorb up to its breaking point is a reflection of its *toughness*.

Woods which can absorb a high amount of non-recoverable strain, and so bend a lot before breaking gradually, are tough woods. Woods which do not do this, but break abruptly with little bending, are brittle (or brash) woods. (Brittleness can also be caused by incorrect seasoning.)

Toughness depends on the strength and elasticity of wood. It is more difficult to break a wood

27

Wooden structural arches in Westminster Hall. This roof was built in 1339 by Richard II

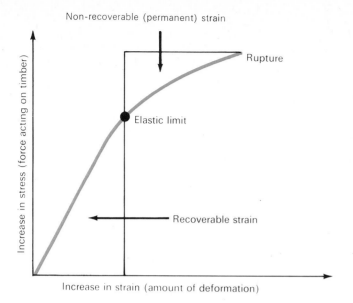

Non-recoverable (permanent) strain

Rupture

Elastic limit

Recoverable strain

Increase in stress (force acting on timber)

Increase in strain (amount of deformation)

Graph to show the stress behaviour of wood

which is as strong as another, but more elastic.

If a stress is applied to wood for a long time permanent deformation results. The wood is said to 'creep' and move away from the load. Wood 'creep' may be observed in the sagging roofs of old buildings.

Clearly there is more to the mechanical properties of wood than a superficial awareness of bending, breaking and hardness. The term hardness is in fact rather meaningless when applied to timber, since the only real hardness of structure in wood is that of the cell wall material. This has hardness of about 2·5 on the geologists' scale of hardness.

Much of timber is made up of empty cell cavities and these give the material a porous nature which affects gross tests of 'hardness'. Nevertheless the term is applied to wood and usually refers to the resistance of timber to indentation. It may also refer to the ease of working or to the way wood

stands up to abrasion. Definition is perhaps of no great significance, but it is as well to remember that children testing the 'hardness' of wood are investigating something which is not clear cut.

## 4.4 Thermal and electrical properties

### Thermal properties
The thermal conductivity of a piece of wood depends on:

a. Grain direction. The conductivity is greatest along the grain.

b. Moisture content. The conductivity is reduced by one-third if the mc is below thirty per cent.

c. Density of the wood. The greater the density the higher the conductivity.

The thermal conductivity of wood is very low compared with, say, metals and its low heat transmission rate explains why wood feels 'warm' to the touch. (Body heat is not quickly transmitted away through the wood.)

Since wood is a poor conductor of heat it is a *good thermal insulator.*

When heated, wood, like any other material, expands, but the thermal expansion of wood is very small and for practical purposes it can be ignored. The very small expansion and contraction of wood material caused by normal changes of the atmospheric temperature are masked by the swelling and shrinkage of wood associated with changes in the moisture content of air at different temperatures.

### The burning of wood
*Wood ignites at about 270 °C* (the exact temperature depends on the chemical nature of different woods) if it is in contact with an unlimited supply of air. If the air supply is limited, ignition does not take place, but the wood material breaks down and gases are driven off by

the heat—a process known as destructive distillation.

The speed with which wood ignites depends on the rate of accumulation of heat at its surface. This is affected by :

a. The size and shape of the wood.

b. The rate of heat loss to the interior of the wood.

c. The rate at which heat is supplied.

Small pieces of wood, having a large surface area exposed to air (eg square splinted matches), are easy to ignite, because of the relatively small amount of heat necessary to raise the temperature of the whole piece to its ignition point.

Large pieces of wood are much slower to catch fire because the conduction of heat to the interior keeps the surface temperature below ignition temperature. However, if heat at a fairly low temperature is maintained for a long time, ignition will occur when the entire piece is eventually raised to its ignition temperature. This may take considerable time, since the slow heating of the surface causes the wood to char and the charred material acts as an insulator to the rapid flow of heat to the interior.

Man has used burning wood as a fuel from the earliest of times. The fuel value of a piece of wood—that is, the amount of heat energy released when it burns—depends on the density of the wood and the amount of water it contains.

When wood is heated in steam it will bend. Man makes use of this fact when he produces such things as tennis racket frames.

**Electrical properties**
Really dry wood is an excellent electrical insulating material.

The conduction of electricity through wood is dependent on its moisture content. The wetter the wood the more its electrical conductivity increases, until at the point where it is completely saturated with moisture its conductivity approaches that of water.

Man makes use of this property in the electrical determination of the moisture content of wood. He uses a calibrated instrument which determines the resistance of a piece of wood to an electrical current, and so can 'read off' its moisture content.

Wood used for high-voltage instrument panels is impregnated with synthetic resins to make it waterproof and so reduce its electrical conductivity.

When wood is subjected to alternating current (ac) the wall materials behave in an interesting way. The molecules orientate themselves to the direction of the electric field and change direction when the direction of the field changes. At low current frequencies the movement of the molecules is very slow, but at very high frequencies the oscillation of the molecules is very rapid. The molecules move so rapidly against each other that a considerable amount of frictional heat is produced. This property is used by man in the radio frequency heating of wood for setting glue lines in furniture.

## 4.5 Properties related to the use of timber

Wood is very versatile—indeed were it possible to manufacture a synthetic substance of equal versatility it would be hailed as a wonder.

No other material is used as a fuel source, a source material for the chemical industry *and* as a structural material.

Timber scores over other materials on account of its general availability and the fact that, unlike metals, it is a replaceable substance.

As a structural material it meets stiff competition from other materials but is superior in certain properties.

This old dhow is a fine example of using wood functionally and aesthetically

a. Unlike metals, for example, it can be cut and worked by simple hand tools; it may be joined by simple techniques of nailing, screwing, bolting or gluing. These factors make 'on the site' use comparatively simple.

b. Wood is the only major structural material which combines good strength properties with good insulating properties:
Heat loss through bricks is about six times as great as through timber.
Heat loss through glass is about eight times as great as through timber.
Heat loss through concrete is about fifteen times as great as through timber.
Heat loss through steel is about 350 times as great as through timber.

c. Wood has an excellent mechanical strength to weight ratio. It combines lightness with strength and on a weight for weight basis is as strong as commercial steel.

d. Its thermal properties make it a valuable building material. It has good insulating properties and structural timbers do not quickly collapse in fires. Wooden beams burn slowly, because the surface chars and reduces oxygen flow to the wood. They lose their stability slowly without marked expansion and change of shape; metal beams will expand considerably and this may cause the collapse of a building.

e. Wood does not deteriorate appreciably if protected from rot, since the major constituents of wood are quite inert to the action of many chemicals.

f. Wood has a wide variation in appearance and is a material with considerable aesthetic appeal.

Against all these advantages one must set the disadvantages:

a. The hygroscopic nature of wood renders it more liable than other materials to dimensional changes caused by changing conditions of humidity.

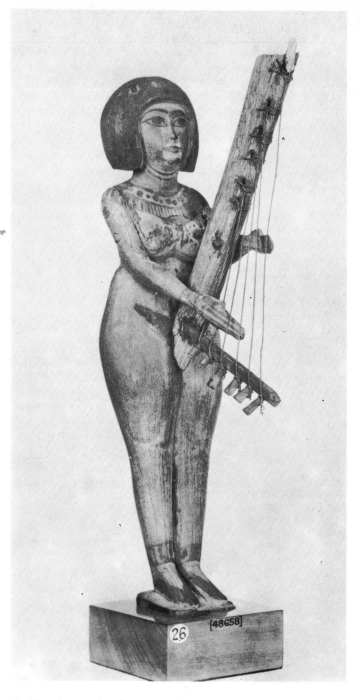

An Egyptian wooden figure approximately 3000 years old

A section of bat-willow tree after having been cut and split into sizes for cricket bat making

b. Wood, like all natural materials, is not a uniform substance; it varies in structure and properties:

Timber from different kinds of trees varies.

Timber from trees of the same kind varies according to conditions of growth, and hereditary factors.

Timber from the same tree varies in relation to annual growth, the vertical position of the wood and the age of the wood.

Nevertheless, if these disadvantages are understood, timber can be suitably specified for use. The structure of wood makes it a valuable material for man and it is perhaps significant that Professor Gordon, in his book *The New Science of Strong Materials*, states:

'it now seems very possible that the coming new engineering materials will resemble much improved versions of wood and bone more closely than they will the metals'.

## Man's choice of timber for particular uses

The selection of a particular timber for a particular use is governed by two main considerations: its suitability for the purpose required, and its cost.

In general, man selects for use the most suitable timber consistent with its cost.

Several factors affect the cost of timber:

*Availability.* It is usually true that the rarer the wood, the more it costs.

*Source.* If the growing trees are easily accessible, easily felled and sawn, and easily transported, the timber tends to be cheaper than that involving high handling and transport charges.

*Ease of working.* Certain timbers work easily and so tend to be cheaper than others which may require more specialist handling. For example, some timbers contain certain deposits which make sawing and constructional operations difficult; others show such variation in properties that their preparation for use is a highly skilled job.

Pit props

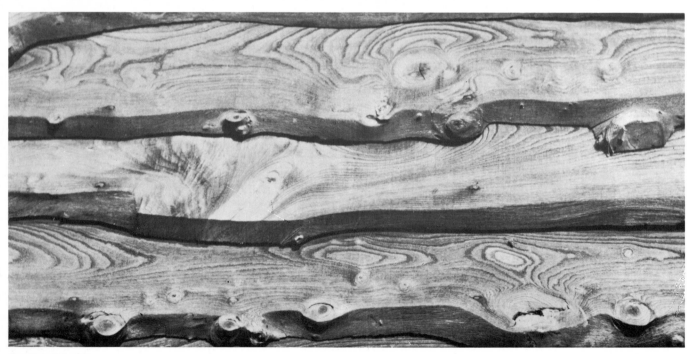

Roofing shingles

*Ease of treatment before final use.* Timbers which require careful seasoning or complex preservative treatment before use tend to be more expensive than others which do not require such treatment.

These are very general points, and clearly the final cost of a particular timber is affected by a combination of all these factors.

Although cost is important when man selects timber for use, it is obviously not just a matter of choosing the cheapest wood. It is necessary to consider what properties are required of a timber if it is to be used in a particular way. Such questions as 'does it look attractive?' 'will it stand up to changing atmospheric conditions?', 'how will it react to mechanical stress?' are important. Some examples may be relevant.

It is impossible in this booklet to consider in great detail all examples and aspects of man's selection of wood; those we have chosen illustrate how the properties of a timber relate to the use man makes of it.

| Use | Required properties | Suitable timber |
| --- | --- | --- |
| Pit props | Above all else the wood must have a high resistance to end grain compression and a high amount of non-recoverable strain to bend slowly before failure (see 4.3) | All conifers except western red cedar, which has low resistance to compression stress |
| Railway sleepers | Resistance to across-the-grain compression and durability in damp conditions | Pine, which has good compression strength and suitable for easy application of preservative |
| Food containers | Lightness with strength, odourless and, to a lesser extent, clean-looking wood | Poplar Sweet chestnut |
| Sports goods, handles and shafts of tools | Resistance to impact, lightness with strength, stability in use | Ash Willow |
| Roofing shingles | Durability in damp conditions, easy cleavage of the wood | Western red cedar |
| Decorative flooring | Good resistance to abrasion and impact, easy application of surface treatments, not excessively noisy, visually acceptable | Oak Beech Hornbeam Maple |

# 5 Defects in timber

In any constructional work it is important to know as accurately as possible the properties of the wood we use. Such questions as 'how much weight will this beam support?' or 'how will this jetty stand up to continual blows from ships docking?' are vital ones, whose neglect could cause costly damage and possible loss of life.

In the previous section we explained briefly why it is difficult to predict with accuracy the properties of 'clean' timber. Prediction is even more difficult when dealing with timber which is not 'clean' but contains defects. All designers and specifiers, in the course of their work, have to make full allowance for any defect which might be present in the wood they deal with, since defects can seriously alter its properties.

Commercial timber is graded with respect to its defects. In the United Kingdom six grades operate. Grade I timber has no visible defects; the lowest Grade VI has visible defects which make it unsuitable for constructional use. Grading rules differ from mill to mill and country to country and experts involved in the buying, selling and distribution of timber have to know how the grading system of one country relates to that used by another. The following table illustrates the variety of grading classes; it is included as a further example of the complexity of the timber trade—a complexity unknown to the layman but one which must be mastered by timber specialists if the wood employed in our day-to-day living is to be safe and adequate for whatever purpose it is used for.

| Use of timber | Grades | | | |
| --- | --- | --- | --- | --- |
| | UK | Finland and Sweden | Russia | Canada |
| High-class joinery | I | — | — | Clear |
| General joinery | II | Unsorted (U/S) | Unsorted (U/S) | Selected Merchantable |
| General building | III | Fifths (V) | Fourths (IV) | Merchantable |
| Packing cases and low-grade constructional work | IV | VI (Utskott) | VI (Utskott) | Common |

Until recently all grading was done visually : defects were noted by eye and the timber assigned to an appropriate grade. Such a system has its limitations since it does not take into account any defects which cannot be seen.

Recently machines have been developed for the electronic grading of timber and it is now possible to 'stress grade' timber with respect to all defects, visible and unseen. Any hidden defects cause a signal to be sent back from the wood which is different from that received from clean wood. The process has far-reaching implications, for it enables us to specify timber with very great accuracy.

Defects in timber may originate in the natural growth of a tree ; they may occur as a result of faulty seasoning, or they may be caused by an attack from living things.

## 5.1 Natural defects

Most people are aware of the knots that occur in wood and in many houses knotted timber, such as Scots pine, is put to decorative use. Yet knots are a defect if wood is used for constructional purposes. They are perhaps the most obvious of all timber defects, but many others exist. Some, with intriguing names, such as shakes, splits, cross grain and gum pockets, are easily visible ; others—for example, brashness, reaction wood, tension and compression wood—need a trained eye for their detection and are best left to timber technologists.

### Knots
Knots are caused by branches. The British Standards Institution defines a knot as 'a section of a branch which has been embedded in the wood by the natural growth of the tree'.

Each branch begins in the centre of a tree and when the trunk is cut into planks the saw passes through embedded portions of branches.

As long as a branch bears leaves and so continues to grow, its cambium cells (2.1) are continuous with those of the trunk. Each year a new layer of cells is added to trunk and branch alike, with the result that both increase in girth at the same time and their covering of bark is gradually increased to form a continuous protective layer over the whole tree. A saw cut through an embedded portion of a branch that has grown in this manner will show a knot in which the outer rings of the branch are fused with the adjoining rings of the trunk wood. Such a knot, bonded into the surrounding wood, is called a *sound* (or live) knot.

However, branches on a living tree are liable to lose their leaves ; the ends of a branch may be broken off or the leaves may drop off when they are gradually excluded from light by the dense foliage on branches above them. In these circumstances no further growth of the branch occurs. The trunk, on the other hand, continues to expand and gradually grows to envelop the branch *together with the bark surrounding it*. The bark surrounding the branch forms a dividing line between the wood of the branch and the wood of the trunk. Thus, when a saw cuts through a branch that has been enclosed in this manner, it produces a knot separated from the rest of the wood by a line equivalent to the thickness of the bark. Such a knot, separated from the surrounding wood is called a *dead* knot. Sometimes the separation results in looseness (*loose* knot) ; sometimes there is no looseness, although a definite line of demarcation between the knot and the surrounding wood can be seen (*tight* knot).

Occasionally, a tree branch breaks off (eg by storm damage), leaving a jagged stump. The stump usually collects moisture and becomes infected with fungus. As a result it dies and rots and when enclosed by wood from the growing stump it remains as an area of soft, brittle wood. If a saw cuts through this area it exposes a *rotten* knot.

All the knots described are named on the basis of how tightly the knot bonds to the adjacent wood.

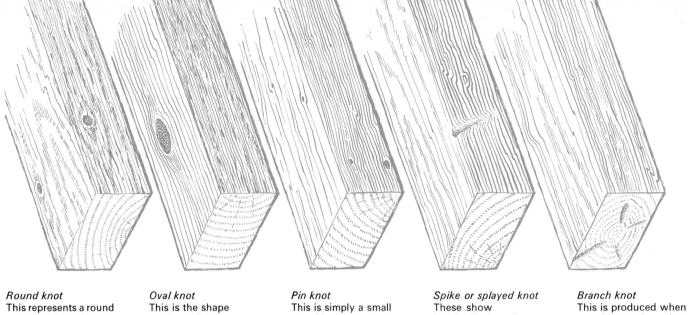

*Round knot*
This represents a round cross-section of the branch on the face or edge of a plank

*Oval knot*
This is the shape produced by a diagonal cut across the branch

*Pin knot*
This is simply a small round knot

*Spike or splayed knot*
These show longitudinal sections through the branch

*Branch knot*
This is produced when wood is cut through a point from which several branches have developed

Knots may also be described by their shape.

Knots can be a serious defect in timber, since they weaken the wood. The strength of wood is related to grain direction (see 4.3) and when knots are formed the grain in the region of a knot is seriously distorted.

## 5.2 Defects caused by faulty seasoning

When wood is seasoned it is dried to the required moisture content (see 4.2). The seasoning process must be carefully controlled in order that the wood loses moisture gradually. If uneven drying occurs, cracks and splits may result. Wood cells differ markedly in the nature and thickness of their walls, and as timber dries shrinkage of the cells (4.2) occurs at different rates in different cells. As a result,

stresses are set up in the wood and large cracks or *shakes* may occur.

Shakes reduce the amount of timber in a log and can give rise to mechanically weak wood.

These defects show themselves as a result of seasoning processes but it must be remembered that the real cause of the defect is often related to conditions in the tree from which the wood was obtained. For instance, cup shake may originate in the parting of growth rings during high winds.

## 5.3 Defects caused by living organisms

The chemical nature of wood is such that it provides a food source for certain living organisms which, as a result of their activities, are responsible for changes in woody material.

## IMPORTANT WOOD-DESTROYING BEETLES

| Beetle and Larva | Chiefly attacks | Nature of tunnels |
|---|---|---|
| *House Longhorn* <br> 25 mm | Seasoned softwoods only — particularly roofing timber | Contain coarse dust with cylindrical pellets (frass) |
| *Powder-post* <br> 5 mm | Sapwood of hardwoods only <br><br> Serious pest of timber yards | Contain dust which is flour-like when rubbed between fingers |
| *Furniture* <br> 3 mm | Softwoods and hardwoods and some plywoods <br><br> Causes woodworm in structural timbers and furniture | Contain gritty dust with cigar-shaped frass |
| *Deathwatch* * <br> 6 mm | Hardwoods, especially oak, if the wood is partially decayed by fungus <br><br> (Confined to old buildings) | Contain gritty dust with bun-shaped frass |

The organisms which attack timber, and often seriously affect its properties, are those which are able to feed on wood. This is a rather specialised kind of nutrition and it is not surprising that the animals and plants involved are representatives of but a few of the numerous existing groups of living things.

In Britain, although certain bacteria are responsible for staining timber, and certain molluscs may badly affect wood submerged in sea water, most damage to timber is caused by insects and fungi.

## Damage caused by insects

In Britain many millions of pounds are lost each year as a result of timber damage caused by insect attack. This is a problem, but it is a small-scale one in comparison with the timber losses encountered in the tropics, where the climatic conditions favour the activities of a wider range of pests—the termites being the most spectacular of all timber destroyers.

Damage in Britain is mainly caused by beetles, and there are three important groups to consider: longhorn beetles; powder-post beetles; furniture beetles.

All have a life cycle which is basically identical, but may vary in time span from group to group.

All the beetles described above cause defects in timber because of their wood-eating habits. There is another group of beetles—the pinhole borers—which may cause damage to freshly felled wood and so disfigure converted timber. 'Pinholing' is merely a visual defect; the affected timber is perfectly sound for constructional purposes. The female lays eggs in cracks in the wood. With each batch of eggs she deposits a fungal spore. If the moisture content of the wood remains high, the fungus develops and is eaten by the beetle larvae when they hatch. The larvae do not eat wood.

Furniture and structural timbers can be extensively damaged as a result of beetle attack and it is natural to think of the beetles as exclusive pests of buildings. Yet they can also affect forest

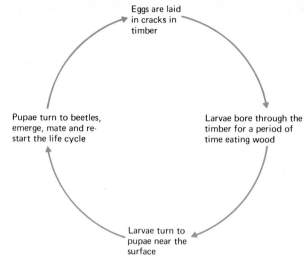

The basic life-cycle of wood damaging beetles

timber. Indeed, it is as well to remember that insects were attacking wood long before man began to use it for structural and decorative purposes.

## Damage caused by fungi

Unlike green plants, which are able to make their own food, all fungi require a supply of manufactured food and in the case of timber-damaging fungi this supply comes from the timber itself.

There are two types of attack from fungi:

(a) Wood-rotting fungi convert the wood substance into food. (These are economically the more important.)

(b) Sap-staining fungi feed only on the cell contents of sapwood.

For a rot to develop and flourish it requires: food (supplied by the wood), water and air. Remove any of these and the fungus will die.

Basically the life cycle of each rot is the same.

There are many species of rot, and the two best known in Britain are *dry rot* and *wet rot*.

Roof timbers can be completely destroyed by the house longhorn beetle, though still apparently sound on the surface

**Dry rot** *(Merulius lacrymans)* is so called because it leaves the wood in a very dry, friable condition. The wood can be crushed between finger and

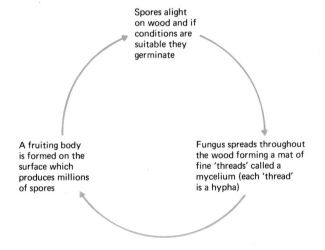

Spores alight on wood and if conditions are suitable they germinate

Fungus spreads throughout the wood forming a mat of fine 'threads' called a mycelium (each 'thread' is a hypha)

A fruiting body is formed on the surface which produces millions of spores

The basic life-cycle of wood rotting fungi

thumb to a fine reddish-brown powder.

An attack of dry rot, if not discovered, will cause extensive damage to a building. It attacks places where water has been allowed to gather on wood but the wood is not permanently wet. Leaking pipes, kitchen and bathroom condensation may result in dry rot if the ventilation is poor. Very often the rot is only found when someone or something falls through a floor, although signs of attack are often noticeable earlier—a musty mushroom smell and red dust gathering under carpets or on floors.

Dry rot will not attack in dry conditions, but once it has started it can produce its own water supply and extend to attack timber that is perfectly dry. The name *lacrymans*, or weeping, comes from this fact and water can be seen dripping from the growth. Dry rot is difficult to eradicate. It can penetrate through brickwork from one building to another and its cure requires technical advice. All defective timber must be removed and apparently sound timber must be cut away at least 600 mm from the last signs of decay. Neighbouring brickwork must be burnt off and treated with fungicidal plugs and all tools and objects in contact with the rotting wood must be sterilised. After this drastic treatment the whole area must be well ventilated to prevent further attack.

**Wet rot** is not as serious as dry rot and the attack takes place only where there is a continual supply of water; very often this occurs in cellars, hence its alternative name of cellar rot. If its water supply is removed the fungus will die, although its spores may remain in the air for a considerable period of time.

Wet rot is much easier to treat than dry rot. All that is required is to thoroughly ventilate the area and to stop the supply of water.

Rots can be prevented by the use of naturally durable timbers, with a moisture content below twenty percent, that are kept well ventilated.

Numerous rots occur on standing timber, but their description is out of the scope of this book.

Fruiting body of dry rot. It produces millions of spores, each of which could spread and develop if conditions are suitable

## 5.4 Durability and preservation of timber

### Durability of timber
Natural durability refers to the resistance wood has to decay when it is in moist conditions.

Timbers vary greatly in their natural durability and are classified according to the number of years they remain durable when in contact with the ground.

In general, heartwood is more durable than sapwood, and the deeper the colour of the heartwood, the more durable it is.

### Preservation of timber
Timbers vary greatly in their natural resistance to decay. The object of preservation techniques is to increase the resistance of timber, ie to increase its durability.

Preservation may be achieved by a variety of methods. In some situations wood may be used with its protective bark left on. Sometimes wood in contact with damp conditions is charred as a preservative measure—a method little used now but common in the past (the Romans charred house foundations). Today preservation normally refers to the treatment of wood by solutions which make it poisonous to pests and fungi.

(a) Types of preservative used. There are three main classes:

Class TO—Tar oil type, eg creosote.
Class OS—Organic solvent type, eg protim.
Class WR—Water-borne type, eg tanalith.

(b) Methods of applying preservative. The choice of method depends on such things as:

The kind of timber to be treated (timbers differ in their resistance to impregnation by preservative).

The span of durability required.

The cost of the application process.

| Durability | Life in contact with ground | Examples of home-grown timbers |
| --- | --- | --- |
| Durable | 15–25 years | Oak (heartwood)<br>Western red cedar (heartwood)<br>Chestnut (heartwood) |
| Moderately durable | 10–15 years | Japanese larch (heartwood)<br>European larch (heartwood)<br>Douglas fir (heartwood) |
| Non-durable | 5–10 years | Elm<br>Almost all softwoods<br>(except western red cedar,<br>Japanese and European larch,<br>Douglas fir) |
| Perishable | Less than 5 years | Sapwood from all species<br>Heartwood of all common<br>hardwoods (except oak,<br>chestnut, elm) |

Some preservatives (used because of their poisonous effect on fungi and insects) may also be harmful to man. It is important to remember this and examine carefully any preservative that might be used by children.

| Method of application | Method used for | Penetration of preservative |
| --- | --- | --- |
| **PRESSURE** Timber placed in a metal cylinder and preservative forced into timber under pressure | Most timbers Sapwood of all timbers | Complete penetration of sapwood. Good penetration of heartwood |
| **HOT AND COLD OPEN TANK TREATMENT** Timber in tank of preservative which is heated; timber then either left in preservative as it cools or transferred to a tank of cold preservative | Permeable timbers Sapwood of all timbers | Deep sapwood penetration. Some penetration of heartwood |
| **COLD DIPPING AND STEEPING** Timber immersed in cold preservative | Permeable timbers and sapwood of all timbers | Penetration depends largely on immersion time and permeability of timber |
| **DIFFUSION** Carried out only on timber freshly felled and sawn Timber is immersed in preservative, then close piled to allow preservative to spread through the wood | Softwood timbers under carefully controlled conditions | Almost complete penetration |
| **BRUSH AND SPRAYING** Surface application of preservative | For timber used in situation where deep preservation not required | Surface protection and some penetration of sapwood |

# 6 Wood products

Man makes use of wood in an enormous number of ways. He uses it in its solid state, and also converts it into other things. The uses of solid timber are so obvious that they are excluded from this section. We are concerned here with wood products, ie things made from wood, in which the wood takes on a different form from that of solid timber.

For convenience we may divide such products into those made in such a way that the woody cells remain basically unaltered (direct products); and those made in such a way that the woody structure is chemically altered (derived products).

## 6.1 Direct products

### Veneers and plywoods
The art of veneering, or using very thin sheets of timber, is an ancient one and we can see many fine examples in antique furniture where the technique is sometimes used to make beautiful and often scarce wood go a long way by sticking it on to plain wood.

Thin sheets of wood are now used extensively in the production of plywoods. Essentially plywood is obtained by sticking three or more thin sheets of wood together. The sheets or veneers may be obtained by peeling or slicing logs which have been softened by hot water or steam treatment. Plywood is made by sticking separate veneers together. In most plywoods the grains of the veneers are used at right angles to each other (an arrangement that has important effects on its properties—see 4).

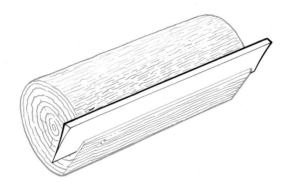

*Slicing*
This is a method of cutting thin sheets of highly decorative or rare wood. The log is held firmly on a moving belt and pushed forward on to a sharp knife blade

*Peeling*
This is carried out by holding a log firmly, revolving it at speed and moving a knife blade forward until it is in contact with the log. In this way a continuous veneer is produced which can be cut to the required size

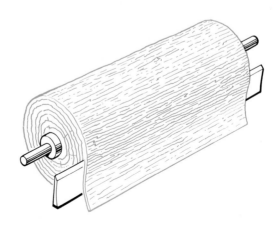

Blockboard above, Laminboard below

Plywoods may be described by the number of veneers in their make-up, eg 3, 5, 9 ply; by their thickness; or by the kind of adhesive used to join the veneers together. They may also be referred to as internal or external use plywoods (this distinction is based on the suitability of the adhesive for use in dry or wet conditions), or classed as MR (moisture resistant) and WBP (weather and boil proof). WBP plywood is capable of withstanding seventy-two hours' immersion in boiling water without separating into its component veneers.

*Advantages of plywoods.* Their particular construction makes them free from all the disadvantages of unidirectional grain. They are strong in all directions and do not warp.

They can be made into larger sheets than can be obtained from wood cut from trees.

### Laminboard and blockboard
These are composed of blocks of wood between two outer veneers and have the same advantages as plywood in use.

### Chipboard
As the name implies, this is made from small chips of wood. The chips are normally made from logs set aside for the purpose (frequently logs which are too small for conversion). The wood is mechanically broken down into chips of the required size which are mixed with adhesives, spread in special machines and pressed into flat boards.

Since the adhesives used are not of WBP standard, chipboard is unsuitable for use out of doors. In other respects it has the advantages of plywood.

### Fibreboards
These are made from wood which has been broken up by grinding it against special stones. (The process is known as mechanical pulping.)

As a result of this pulping the wood is reduced to tiny fibres which are stuck together under pressure to form fibreboards. Hardboard and insulating board are both fibreboards made in this manner, but hardboard is compressed to a greater degree.

### Wood 'wool'
A direct product used as a packing material for delicate objects. It is the 'shreddings' of carefully selected timber produced on special machines in such a way that the 'wool' has a greater resilience than ordinary shavings.

### Wood 'flour'
As its name suggests, a flour-like form of wood produced by a special mechanical process. It is used in the manufacture of plastics.

## 6.2 Derived products

These are derived from wood by chemical treatment. Such treatment may involve complex chemical reactions and details of the various processes are not relevant here.

The following table indicates the main processes involved and some common things which utilise derived wood products in their manufacture.

| Process | Treatment given to wood | Resultant products are used in the manufacture of |
|---|---|---|
| Acid hydrolysis | Wood substances are treated with acid | Sugars<br>Cattle food<br>Yeast<br>Adhesives |
| Chemical pulping | Wood is mechanically pulped with chemicals used to assist its breakdown | Paper<br>Rayon<br>Films<br>Plastics<br>Lacquers<br>Cellophane<br>Explosives |
| Destructive distillation | Wood is heated in the absence of air | Charcoal<br>Medicine<br>Poultry food<br>Soap<br>Disinfectants<br>Paints and varnishes<br>Turpentine<br>Acetic Acid<br>Methanol<br>Acetone |
| Extraction | Wood is treated with water and other solvents to dissolve out certain extracts | Soaps<br>Paints<br>Varnishes<br>Dyes<br>Tannins |

# Teachers' bibliography

There are very few books written for the layman which are specifically concerned with wood. It is for this reason we have produced our book of background information as a digest of specialised knowledge.

For teachers who wish to pursue the subject in greater depth we recommend the following books, suggesting that they are best initially obtained through a library.

Edlin, H. L., *Trees, Wood and Man*, New Naturalist Series, Collins.
Desch, H. E., *Timber: Its Structure and Properties*, 4th edition, Macmillan.
Henderson, *Timber: Its Properties, Pests and Preservation*, Lockwood.
Gordon, J. E., *New Science of Strong Materials*, Penguin.
James, N. D. G., *The Forester's Companion*, Blackwell.
TRADA, *Timber Pests and their Control*, publication TBL 25.
Latham, B., *Wood from Forest to Man*, Harrap.
*Encyclopaedia Britannica*.

At a more general level the following pamphlets may prove helpful.

*Forestry in England, Forestry in Scotland, Forestry in Wales* (obtainable at a small cost from the Forestry Commission, 25 Savile Row, London W1).

*The New World of Timber Engineering, Plywood for Building and Construction*. Single copies supplied free to teachers by the Timber Trade Federation of the United Kingdom, Clareville House, Whitcombe Street, London WC2H 7DL. The Timber Trade Federation regret that they cannot supply in bulk.

# Index

**Illustration acknowledgements:**

The publishers gratefully acknowledge the help given by the following in supplying photographs on the pages indicated:

Barnaby's Picture Library, vi, 16, 33, 34
The trustees of the British Museum, 32
Council of the Forest Industries of British Columbia, 10–11
Forest Products Research Laboratory, 2, 3, 4, 5
High Commissioner for New Zealand, 12
Ministry of Culture and National Guidance, Aden, 31
Ministry of Public Building and Works, 28
M. Nimmo, 8
Timber Trade Federation, 8, 27, 46

Line drawings by Colin Rattray

Cover design by Peter Gauld

ISBN 0 356 04010 0